PROPHETIC RAIN

D1557536

PROPHETESS TAMMY JAÉ

PROPHETIC RAIN
by Tammy Jaé

Published by One Faith Publishing

Richmond, VA

onefaithpublshings@gmail.com

PROPHETIC

"My doctrine shall drop as the rain, my speech shall distill as the dew, as the small rain upon the tender herb, and as the showers upon the grass" Deuteronomy 32:2

RAIN

"I'm going to make them and everything that surrounds my hill a blessing. I'll send down the rain! At the appropriate time, there will be a rainstorm of blessing!" Ezekiel 34:26, ISV

I dedicate this book to
The only One who picked me up, dusted me off,
and called me His own. You are the Author and Finisher
of my
Faith.
You are my First Love, my Last Love,
and my All in All.
I love You, Abba Father because You first loved me.
Your daughter, Tammy

TESTIMONIALS

Sylvester Q.

This book is designed for Christians like me because it was knowledgeable and easy to read. It gave me a better understanding of God's strategies against the enemy's tactics. This is an encouraging book that both the young and old saints of God can use to decree and declare the Word of God.

Prophetess Tammy motivates the reader to use God's Word to help encourage yourself. Also, the book was used in my church to teach Bible study to empower and inspire the people of God. I appreciate her diligent work on this book and the next one to come. Prophetess Tammy is a humble and empowering woman of God.

Lisa M.

Overall, this book is absolutely wonderful! Written in a format that is easy to read, straight to the point, and powerful. I recommend Prophetic Rain to anyone that is struggling with their beliefs, rejection, self -pity or feeling lonely in any way. This book is encouraging and insightful! I found myself being molded and restored in various ways, and I learned how to re-gain a consistent prayer life.

Veronica C.

Prophetic Rain has blessed me tremendously, especially during a difficult time. For years, I had been praying without any boldness or authority. Within a few days of reading Prophetic Rain, I saw a mighty move of God in my strength, understanding, and finances.

HEBREWS 4:12

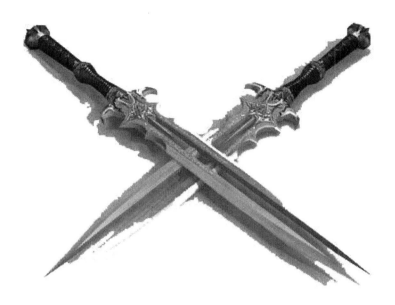

"For the word of God is alive and powerful. It is sharper than the sharpest two-edged sword, cutting between soul and spirit, between joint and marrow. It exposes our innermost thoughts and desires."

TABLE OF CONTENTS

Oftentimes, a reader will skip pass the "Introduction" and right into the chapters, but I'm asking you please to read the entirety of the introduction before moving on to the strategic prayers. By not doing so, you will miss some vital information that's urgently needed.

INTRODUCTION

Are you currently experiencing a season of spiritual drought?

You may be wondering, what is a spiritual drought? Well, allow me to explain.

- A drought (*also known as a dry season*) is a spiritual season where everything in your life is decreasing and nothing seems to be increasing.

- Somehow, all your resources have dried up and withered away.

- It's a season where you feel exhausted from running, but you never reached the finish line.

- Last but not least, you feel weary, stagnated, confused, disappointed, and your ears seem dull to the voice of God.

My friend and Sibling in Christ (S.I.C.), you are not alone!

It's no coincidence that you picked up this book. Yes, the book's title or cover may have caught your attention, but whatever the truth may be, I believe there is a fight sparring inside you - a fight to overcome a struggling season that seems to be a losing battle for many.

At this very moment, a mass amount of believers is experiencing a drought season. Unfortunately, a great many of those believers don't have a clue as to why. This is why I stated earlier, *"You are not alone!"*

It's heartbreaking to say, but quite a few Christians lose their faith during this season, mainly because they do not have a spiritual game plan for survival. Remember, soldiers don't go to war without a game plan. Without a basic understanding of a drought season, there will be a constant battle against the Three-Ds: *disappointment, discouragement,* and *despair.* This battle against the Three-Ds continues to overpower numerous Christians, mostly because a drought is not a popular topic that is often talked about.

We've heard many sermons about the blessings in an over-flow season, but a dry season is rarely taught during Bible study or preached during a Sunday morning sermon on the pulpit, which leaves us without a defense. Without any knowledge of a drought, our twisted thinking will begin to question or blame God as to why He allowed misfortune in our lives. Meanwhile, Satan recognizes that we lack simple knowledge of a drought, and that is when the Three-Ds are sent out on a mission to attack and destroy our faith.

Here's the Top-Secret most Christians miss:

Question: What is the only weapon that overpowers Satan and his imps?

Answer: **The Word of God!**

When Satan tried to tempt Jesus in the wilderness, Jesus counterattacked by simply saying, *"It is written..."* nothing more, and nothing less, but guess who received the victory? Jesus! Yes, it's just that easy. Satan has no authority over the Word of God! (read Matthew 4:1-11)

My friend, you're going to need God's Word to fight your battles because His Word is sharper than any two-edged sword.

Take note and always remember, the Word of God is a sword that slashes Satan every time you use it, and your faith is a shield that protects you against his vicious attacks. (Ephesians 6:11-17). Your spiritual armor is necessary for defeating the Three-Ds or any other entities.

You see, Satan knows that if he destroys your faith, you will become an open target for him to easily attack you (remember, your faith is a shield). Also, if you don't have faith, your blessings will be hindered.

Always keep in mind, without faith it's impossible to please God (Hebrews 11:6). In order to see God move miraculously in your life, you must have faith.

Now, do you see why your faith is under attack? Satan is a deceiving liar and thief, and one of his goals is to stop you from receiving your blessings.

S.I.C., I encourage you not to allow the Three Ds to weary or defeat you in this season, and whatever comes your way,

DO NOT GIVE UP!

The scripture in **Galatians 6:9 states:**
"And let us not be weary in well doing; for in due season
(a new season), we shall reap if we faint not."

The New Living Translation simply states: "So let's not get tired of doing what is good. At just the

right time we will reap a harvest of blessings if we don't give up."

The sole purpose of this book is to help you defeat the Three-Ds by using God's Word, and in return, you can help someone who has very little or no knowledge of a spiritual drought. But first, I am going to enlighten you on "Why?" we experience a dry season.

When we're in a drought season, we often question God just as Job did, especially when we don't understand God's plan and purpose for our future. As with Job, he lost everything because of Satan, but he didn't know that he had been recommended by God, and he didn't foresee that a drought season was placing him in a position to receive an overflow. Listen, Job received a double portion for his troubles. Hallelujah! If Job had known his dry season was shifting to a season of overflow, it would have been much easier to accept the plans God had for his life.

During my season of a drought, I felt exactly like Job. I was confused, and I felt as though I was looking for an exit out of a maze. Everything around me declined, including my hope, finances, business, health, and relationships. It was too much to handle at once. I was so overwhelmed and discouraged that I decided to give up and throw in the towel because I didn't know how to effectively use the Word of God to fight (*I knew the scriptures, but I didn't know how to use it to win my battles*). I was ready to quit the ministry, my marriage, and I even had thoughts of ending my life. **But God!**

Today, I am genuinely grateful for God's renewed mercy be-cause when I desired to give up, God wanted me to keep pressing on. During my mental, spiritual, physical, and emotional melt-down, God gave me a better understanding of the spiritual seasons. He showed me the purpose of a drought, how to survive the season, and how to shift the atmosphere with His Word.

Before I go any further, let's take a moment to look at the different types of seasons. As you may or may not know, all seasons must change because every season has a great purpose both naturally and spiritually. In fact, Ecclesiastes 3 explains this theory, stating, *there is a season and time for everything*. After I studied the revelation that was given by God, I compared the four natural seasons and their purpose to the four spiritual seasons, and here is what I found:

- **New Beginnings {Spring} – A New Beginning Season is similar to Spring.**

This is a season when new creative ideas, inventions, ministries, businesses, books, etc. are birthing. This is also a time of favor, new opportunities, promotions, open doors, divine connections, and divine friendships.

Basically, you will see new things happening in your life during this season.

- **Labor {Summer} – A Labor Season is similar to Summer.**

A Labor season is when many Christians feel exhausted, especially from helping others. You may feel like you're pouring out and giving your time, money, patience, forgiveness, effort, etc., but no one is pouring or giving back to you. S.I.C., please keep doing what you're doing! This is a season to keep laboring and planting your seeds of good deeds. Take notice of the ants and how they work diligently all summer preparing for their harvest.

If you never plant any seeds in your garden, how would anything grow?

- **Harvest {Fall} – The Harvest Season is similar to Fall.** This is a season with a beautiful array of colors, but this is also a season of gathering. Some of the good deed seeds you planted in your labor months have now grown into a full harvest. I stated some seeds, not all, because we must be cautious not to do a good deed to get recognition from people but only from God. Remember, only what you do in secret will be rewarded openly. (Matthew 6: 1-4)

The Harvest is a season that every Christian enjoys and appreciates.

- **Drought {Winter} – A Drought season is similar to winter.**

During the winter, the cold air causes all growth to cease, and during that time nothing grows, the same way nothing grows during a drought. However, both have a significant purpose. A drought season is when many Christians battle the most. Sadly, the battle is mainly against our minds; if the enemy is able to attack the mind, the body will eventually fall.

- *Keep in thought, we have a human body, which was created from the dirt of the earth; therefore, we also experience the same changes in seasons just as the earth seasons change.*

I'm originally from Michigan. It is a state where winters can be brutal, and no one looks forward to the winter season because it's extremely cold, which has its disadvantages. In the winter months, days are short, nights are longer, and studies have shown that this season can bring on major depression or anxiety. But when we look at winter from a positive perspective, it is a season of timing, shifting, resting, reflection, ceased growth, appreciation, intimacy, and cleansing.

This information may seem irrelevant for now, but here are a few facts about winter:

- **Timing** - Most of our **time** is spent indoors, which allows more intimacy with those we love, and for others, this season can cause loneliness.

- **Patience** - In the winter, it does not look like the flowers or tree buds are ever going to bloom, but beneath the surface, seeds are germinating, so we must be **patient** as this process is taking place.

- **Resting** – The earth needs **rest** too. It has to rejuvenate from its production throughout the year.

- **Reflection** – Winter allows us to take a moment and **reflect** on life itself.

- **Appreciation** – The winter host a major holiday that brings families together to show their love and **appreciation** for each other.

- **Cleansing** - During the winter, the frigid air **cleans** the earth of germs and bacteria.

- **Preparation** - Winter is a time of **preparing** the earth for the newness of spring. In the winter, we are actually preparing and making plans for the arrival of spring.

- **Expectation** – After winter, everyone is **expecting** spring to come, and nothing or no one can stop spring from arriving, except God.

Now the comparison:

While in a drought season, we oftentimes feel depressed, anxious, or alone. Our days seem faint, the long nights are weary, and it looks like all growth around us has stopped. My *S.I.C.*, this may sound insane, but a drought season is all about **preparation** and **expectation!** This is a time to prepare yourself for what God is about to do in your life!

In a drought season, you must **trust** in God's timing, **rest** in His Presence, **reflect** on His Word, **appreciate** His Goodness, and **cleanse** yourself through a consecration. The bottom line is, the Heavenly Father desires more intimacy and oneness with you during this season.

Now, here are a few facts about a spiritual drought:

- **Timing** - God desires more **time** and intimacy with you during a drought.

- **Patience** -You must be **patient** and trust in God's timing, not yours.

- **Resting** - **Rest** and rejuvenate in God; don't be in such a rush to get out of His Presence.

- **Reflection** – **Reflect** on God and spend more quality time in His Word.

- **Appreciation** - **Appreciate** what God has already done and continues to do. **Stop complaining!** Complaints actually prolong a drought season. Remember the children of Israel after they left Egypt. Their 11-day journey to the promised land turned into 40 years because of their murmuring and complaining.

  Don't be like the Israelites!

- **Cleansing** – God wants to rid you of those toxins that are not pleasing to Him and detrimental to you. A drought season is a time for **cleansing** and fasting (consecration). You must let go of anything or anyone that is weighing you down and keeping you from moving forward into your next season.

- **Preparation** – God is **preparing** you for the new by removing the old.

- **Expectation** – This is a time to **expect** that a new season is arriving soon. The only person that can hinder you from moving forward into your next season is you.

Now, do you see the comparison between a winter and a drought?

In a natural drought, the soil looks dry, cracked, and hopeless, but once the rain begins to fall, new sprouts will spring up. My friend, God is doing the exact same thing in your life, whatever has dried up, God is about to cause a new thing to spring forth!

Take a look at the Word of God:

"Behold, I will do a new thing; now it shall spring forth; shall ye not know it? I will even make a way in

the wilderness, and rivers in the desert". -Isaiah 43:19, KJV

The NLT version states: "For I am about to do something new. See, I have already begun! Do you not see it? I will make a pathway through the wilderness. I will create rivers in the dry wasteland."

Isaiah 43:19 is definitely a "Praise Break" scripture for me. I get fired up every time I read it! *I got excited for a moment, but let's continue.* A drought season is a very necessary season be-cause it prepares you for the new.

Question: Have you ever needed to purchase a new sofa?

Did you not remove the old to make room for the new?

It would not be a nice-looking sight to have a brand-new sofa sitting on top of the old sofa, right?

The Bible tells us in Matthew 9:17: *"And no one puts new wine into old wineskins (bottles). For the old skins (bottles) would burst from the pressure, spilling the wine and ruining the skins (bottles). New wine is stored in new wineskins so that both are preserved."*

Basically, what I am saying is this: During a drought, God wants to remove some old things out of your life, so He can replace it with something new, but you must be patient and trust the process. Yes, it gets difficult. Believe me, I know, but I also know that the reward is far greater than the struggle. In fact, God is actually doing us a favor by provoking us to move forward into the promises He has already set before us.

I'm going to need you to take your time while reading this next part. In the winter, you know without a shadow of a doubt that the cold-bitter season will soon pass, and spring will be arriving, right? Well, you must have the same, without a shadow of a doubt faith in God, and believe that this dry season will pass, and your new season will be approaching soon.

SNIPPET

I mentioned earlier about the revelation I received from God, here is the breakdown:

- *First, I was given instructions on what to do, but I had to believe that I could achieve it. I had to acknowledge that I am the daughter of an Almighty King (oftentimes we speak it, but do we really believe it).*

- *Second, I had to accept the authority I had been given through the gift of the Holy Spirit. This was a must in order to speak boldly those things that are not, as though they were.*

- *While I continued to seek God silently in prayer (more listening and less talking), I received prayers from heaven that felt like God was downloading and raining on my spirit at the same time.*

- *After writing down what I heard, I prayed the prayers, and that's when God showed me a vision of fire coming out of my mouth, it looked similar to the fire in a dragon's mouth. I soon noticed in the vision that my boldness actually determined how powerful the flames could get. The LORD revealed to me that the fire symbolized the power in strategic prayers.*

Strategic prayers are targeted prayers that uses the Word of God as its main focus; it's like an arrow that hits the center of a bull's eye.

- *Last, God helped me to understand that a drought season is required for humility (remaining humble), which is substantially needed for our spiritual growth.*

Believe me, a drought season has taught me patience. I have learned to patiently wait until I see the full manifestation of God, instead of complaining. Yes, I know a drought season is tough. However, a dry season is not meant to break you; rather, it is meant to make you. It will strengthen your weakness, enlighten your wisdom, and increase your faith.
It will empower you to stand strong when everything around you is crumbling into pieces.

"Humble yourselves therefore under the mighty hand of God, that He may exalt you in due time." - 1 Peter 5:6

God is up to something, and He is ready to release it mightily in your life!

Question: Are you ready?

Allow me to help you get ready for the shifting! I have covered the reason we experience a drought. Now I want to help you understand how to overcome this season with a victory.

Let's take a quick look at the story of Elijah in 1 Kings 17: 9-16, NLT. Elijah was a prophet whom the LORD used to speak things into existence.

"So, he went to Zarephath. As he arrived at the gates of the village, he saw a widow gathering sticks, and he asked her, "Would you please bring me a little water in a cup?"

"As she was going to get it, he called to her, "Bring me a bite of bread, too."

"But she said, "I swear by the Lord your God that I don't have a single piece of bread in the house. And I have only a handful of flour left in the jar and a little cooking oil in the bottom of the jug. I was just gathering a few sticks to cook this last meal, and then my son and I will die."

" But Elijah said to her, "Don't be afraid!" Go ahead and do just what you've said but make a little bread for me first. Then use what's left to prepare a meal for yourself and your son".

"For this is what the Lord, the God of Israel, says: There will always be flour and olive oil left in your containers until the time when the Lord sends rain and the crops grow again!"

'So, she did as Elijah said, and she and Elijah and her family continued to eat for many days."

"There was always enough flour and olive oil left in the containers, just as the Lord had promised through Elijah".

The moral of the story is: The widow woman was in a drought season, and everything in her village had dried up and withered away. All resources were gone, and she was at the point of throwing in the towel. **But God!** Our Gracious Father, who is full of mercy sent Elijah with a prophetic word. The drought season didn't change, but the widow's circumstances surely did. Even though it was a drought, God supplied her with what she needed to survive. Why? Because she believed the Rhema (right now) Word spoken through Elijah **without fear**. The widow blessed Elijah with the little that she had, and in return, she was blessed with an overflow. S.I.C., I need you to catch what I'm throwing here. She had to get rid of the old flour and oil, so God could overflow her jugs with the new. Hallelujah!

Did you know that God can cause your atmosphere to be shifted from not enough to more than enough?

The keywords that stood out in this passage are **"Don't be afraid!"** In the King James Version, it is written, **"Fear not!"** Do you know that fear is a blocker to any blessing?

Fear will block the Word of God from moving on your behalf. Fear will cause you to doubt what God can do because fear is the opposite of faith.

Fear wants you to stand still, and faith wants you to keep moving forward.

Did the widow choose fear or faith?_____

What caused God to move on her behalf ?_____

That's exactly right, faith. Despite her current situation, she still chose faith because faith, not fear, is what causes God to move on our behalf. Remember what I stated earlier, Satan wants to attack and destroy your faith, and according to scripture, only faith pleases God.

Elijah perceived that the widow was fearful about sharing her last meal, so he encouraged her not to be afraid. My friend, fear and faith do not mix. Fear wants to sabotage what God told you to do, write a book, start a business, ministry, etc., just like fear wanted to sabotage the widow woman from receiving her blessing.

We should not only carry around the fancy title of a Believer, but as "Believers of Christ", we **must also believe** that God can do all things but fail.

Let's take a brief look at another great story of Elijah as he called forth the rain in 1 Kings 18:41-46:

"Then Elijah said to Ahab, "Go get something to eat and drink, for I hear a mighty rainstorm coming!"

"So Ahab went to eat and drink. But Elijah climbed to the top of Mount Carmel and bowed low to the ground and prayed with his face between his knees."

"Then he said to his servant, "Go and look out toward the sea."

"The servant went and looked, then returned to Elijah and said, "I didn't see anything."

"Seven times Elijah told him to go and look.

"Finally the seventh time, his servant told him, "I saw a little cloud about the size of a man's hand rising from the sea."

"Then Elijah shouted, "Hurry to Ahab and tell him, 'Climb into your chariot and go back home. If you don't hurry, the rain will stop you!'"

"And soon the sky was black with clouds. A heavy wind brought a terrific rainstorm..."

S.I.C., I need you to allow this keyword to marinate in your spirit, "**Prayer**".

Elijah bowed his head in prayer and called forth the rain.
S.I.C., do you hear what this scripture is saying? Elijah heard the rain coming in the spiritual realm before his servant saw a drop of rain in the natural. Now that's Powerful!

Let me reassure you that Our God is the same God back then, who spoke through Elijah, blessed the widow woman, and allowed Elijah to stop and call forth the rain.

Did you know that you can do the same thing today through prayer and fasting?

Well, not literally calling on the natural rain but calling on the spiritual blessings of God that fall like rain.

"I will open the windows of heaven for you. I will pour out a blessing so great you won't have enough room to take it in! Try it! Put me to the test!"-Malachi 3:10. NLT

Your God-given rights

Yes, those who walk in the office of a prophet have been graced and gifted with a higher level of prophetic authority like Elijah. However, <u>every child</u> of the Most High God has been graced with power through the gifting of the Holy Spirit (Acts 1:8).

Every Holy Spirit-filled believer has been authorized to shift, decree, declare, speak to dry bones, call forth the rain, and speak things that are not as though they were! This type of authority has been given to all the Father's children at the beginning of creation (Genesis 1:28). It's our God-given rights as royal priesthood and heirs to His Kingdom.

Remember, YOU DO NOT HAVE TO BE A PROPHET OR PROPHETESS TO SPEAK OVER YOUR OWN LIFE!

Get ready! It's time to shift your atmosphere!

I mentioned in the snippet that God poured out specific prayers in my spirit like rain. I have been instructed by God to release those prayers via a book to teach His people how to use His Word to fight their battles. Over the next 21 days, I encourage you to pray the strategic prayers, so you can see the manifestation of God's Power for yourself. I have witnessed the blessings of these prayers because God's Word cannot return to Him. The prayers from "Prophetic Rain" has truly blessed me, and it continues to bless many others. I pray that each prayer will cause you to go deeper in God, which will cause a miraculous divine shifting!

INSTRUCTIONS

Below are a few instructions to follow during the next 21 days of fasting and praying. If you want results, you must do what it takes to receive results.

- Each prayer must be spoken with faith.

Praying without faith is a useless prayer. Its destination is the ceiling, not heaven. Our prayers are meant to shift atmospheres, not just a room.

- Prayers must be spoken with confidence and boldness. You cannot shift an atmosphere praying like a baby, out of fear, or doubt.

- Preferably, pray in the early morning because it will help set the order for the rest of your day. David said, *"Early will I rise and seek You."* -Psalm 63:1

Proverbs 8:17 states: *"I love them that love me, and those that seek me early shall find me."*

- Fast during the next 21 days (abstain from food) during a specific time.

- **Fasting is a prayer booster!**

- Let's be honest. What is your sacrifice? You want something, but what are you willing to give up? Perhaps your favorite foods.

- **Fasting** will also help break any strongholds, barriers, or excess baggage you may be carrying, knowingly or unknowingly.

- A basic 12 am -12 noon fast is suggested for individuals who are new to fasting or taking medications; otherwise, fast from 12 am – 4 pm.

- *"Is not this the fast that I have chosen? to loose the bands of wickedness, to undo the heavy burdens, and to let the oppressed go free, and that you break every yoke?" -Isaiah 58:6*

- I strongly recommend journaling your progress. Write how you feel, your encounters with the Holy Spirit, the shift in the atmosphere, and so forth. Journaling is also a good tool to reflect on at a later time. For your convenience, I have added a few note pages after each prayer to write down your thoughts.

- I also highly recommend that you read this book yearly to help keep you prepared for when a drought season approaches.

- Please note, there is always a strategic order with God. You will notice that the first several prayers are geared towards removing the extra weight and baggage that you may be carrying. Remember, old things must be removed before God can spring forth the new.

- Make a commitment to finish strong!

- Please seek the advice of a healthcare **professional** before fasting, if you have a medical condition. If you have any questions regarding the instructions, the prayers, or testimonies, please forward all emails to PROPHETICRAINPRAYERS@gmail.com

Day 01

RECLAIM YOUR PEACE!

"The Lord will give strength unto his people; the Lord will bless his people with peace."-Psalm 29:11

{Has the adversary stolen your peace and left you with weary days and sleepless nights? If so, it's time to reclaim your peace, today!}

Today, I receive total victory over my Peace, and I take back full possession!

I reclaim and restore every ounce of my Peace, In Yeshua's' Name!

I decree and declare restitution for every weary day and sleepless night that my Peace was stolen!

Satan's demonic culprits! You are the thieves and enemies of Peace.

Today, I serve you notice, you have been illegally and fraudulently possessing my Peace, to which you have no legal rights. All illegal acts against my Peace must cease and desist right now, In the Name of Jesus Christ of Nazareth!

You have been trespassing on unauthorized territory because my body, my mind, my spirit, and my soul belongs to ABBA!

Today, I reinstate my Peace back to its rightful owner,

_____ (your name).

Peace is my birthright!

Peace is my portion!

Peace is my position!

Peace is my inheritance from the Prince of Peace!

My Father Word says in John 14:27: "**Peace I leave with you, My peace I give unto you, not as the world giveth, give I unto you. Let not your heart be troubled, neither let it be afraid.**"

Today, I walk in the PERFECT PEACE that surpasses all understanding!

I have a PERFECT PEACE that gives joy, happiness, love, a sound mind, fearless victory, and an untroubled heart!

And it is so. Amen.

DATE___/____/_____

JOURNAL & NOTES

"In the light of the king's countenance is life; and his favor is as a cloud of the latter rain". Proverbs 16:15

_____

_____

_____

_____

_____

_____

_____

_____

_____

_____

_____

_____

_____

_____

_____

_____

today is: MONTH of _____ YEAR _____

day 1 2 3 4 5 6 7 8 9 10 11 12 13 14 15 16 17 18 19 20 21 22 23 24 25 26 27 28 29 30 31

PRAYER *is your* PERSONAL KEY *to* heaven

BOYD K. PACKER

Today I am grateful for:

prayer journal

I have seen the
Hand of God
in my life today

pray for:
_____
_____
_____
_____
_____
_____
_____
_____
_____
_____
_____
_____
_____
_____

Day 02

I RELEASE

"Do you not know that you are God's temple and that God's Spirit dwells in you?"- 1 Corinthians 3:16, ESV

{When the Spirit of God dwells in you, everything else has to go! You must let go of the old you, so God can begin a new work within you.} -Tammy Jae

Today, I release complaining, and I replace it with a praise of Thanks, according to **1 Thessalonians 5:18: "In everything give thanks; for this is the will of God in Christ Jesus concerning me."**

I release worry, and I replace it with a steadfast mind according to Your Word in **Isaiah 26:3: "You will keep in perfect peace those whose minds are steadfast because they trust in You."**

Right now, I release the characteristics of fear, anxiety, paranoia, and its residue, and I replace it with Your Word in **2 Timothy 1:7: "God has not given me the spirit of fear but of power, and of love, and of a sound mind! Yea, though I walk through the valley of the shadow of death, I will fear no evil because You, Oh Lord are with me!" In the Name of Yeshua!**

I release doubt, and I replace it with a Now Faith! **Hebrew 11:1 states: "Now faith is the substance of things hoped for, the evidence of things not seen."**

Today, I release disappointment, discouragement, and despair, and I replace it with **Philippians 4:7: "The peace of God which passes all understanding shall keep my heart and mind through Christ Jesus."**

Today, I am released from every stronghold of bondage in every area of my life, and I replace it with Your Mighty Hand according to the LORD's Word in **Exodus 6:6: "And I will redeem you with a stretched-out arm."**

In the Mighty Name of Yeshua (Jesus), I pray. Amen.

DATE___/____/_____

JOURNAL & NOTES

"Be glad then, ye children of Zion, and rejoice in the Lord your God: for he hath given you the former rain moderately, and he will cause to come down for you the rain, the former rain, and the latter rain in the first month." -Joel 2:23

_____

_____

_____

_____

_____

_____

_____

_____

_____

_____

_____

_____

_____

today is: MONTH of _____ YEAR _____

day 1 2 3 4 5 6 7 8 9 10 11 12 13 14 15 16 17 18 19 20 21 22 23 24 25 26 27 28 29 30 31

PRAYER
is your
PERSONAL
KEY to
heaven
BOYD K. PACKER

Today I am grateful for:

prayer journal

I have seen the
Hand of God
in my life today

pray for:

Day 03

BIND AND LOOSE

"Truly I tell you, whatever you bind on earth will be bound in heaven, and whatever you loose on earth will be loosed in heaven". -Matthew 18:18, NIV

{This prayer is meant to bind any and everything that is not of God and loose (release) His Holy Word into your life.}

Today, I come in the authority and Name of Jesus Christ to bind and to loose!

I bind every negative confession that I've spoken over my life with my own words, and I loose **Proverbs 16:24: "Pleasant words are as a honeycomb, sweet to the taste and health to my body."**

I bind all negative thinking that tries to affect and manipulate my thoughts, and I loose **2 Corinthians 10:5: "I Cast down imaginations and every high thing that exalted itself against the knowledge of God and bringing into captivity every thought to the obedience of Christ."**

Today, I choose to change my thought pattern according to my Father's Word in **Philippians 4:8: "Whatsoever things are true, whatsoever things are honest, whatsoever things are just, whatsoever things are pure, whatsoever things are lovely, whatsoever things are of good report; if there be any virtue, and if there be any praise, think on these things!"**

I bind every word curse and incantation that was spoken against my life, and I loose **Isaiah 54:17: "No weapon formed against me shall prosper, and every tongue which rises against me in judgment Thou shall condemn."**

In the Name Of Jesus, I bind every fiery arrow that is launched against me, every fiery arrow shall stop, fall, and crumble at my feet because I am covered by the hedge of protection according to **Job 1:10: "Have you not placed a hedge on every side around me, my house, and everything I have."**

I bind every demonic accuser that is sent to destroy my character with false accusations.

I bind every plot and plan sent from the enemy's camp, In Jesus' Name!

I bind all blocking spirits, eavesdropping spirits, demonic interferences, demonic influence, demonic attachments, imitating demons, demonic annihilation, and demonic assassinations that were sent to destroy my purpose and destiny. Only my Heavenly Father holds the blueprint to my beginning and my ending. Right now, I loose **Jeremiah 29:11 over my life: " For I know the thoughts that I think towards you, said the Lord, thoughts of peace and not of evil, to give me an expected end."**

In Jesus' Name. Amen.

DATE____/_____/_____

JOURNAL & NOTES

"Drop down, ye heavens, from above, and let the skies pour
down righteousness: let the earth open, and let them bring
forth salvation, and let righteousness spring up together; I
the LORD have created it."
-Isaiah 45:8

_____

_____

_____

_____

_____

_____

_____

_____

today is: MONTH of _____ YEAR _____

day 1 2 3 4 5 6 7 8 9 10 11 12 13 14 15 16 17 18 19 20 21 22 23 24 25 26 27 28 29 30 31

PRAYER
is your
PERSONAL
KEY to
heaven
BOYD K. PACKER

Today I am grateful for:

prayer journal

I have seen the
Hand of God
in my life today

pray for:

Day 04

I AM FREE!

"If the Son sets you free, you will be free indeed". -John 8:36

{Free yourself from everything the adversary has used to weigh you down. Set yourself free today!}

Today, I am free from a vagabond mindset!

I am released from a wandering mind!

Today, I am free from double-mindedness!

I am released from all unstable thinking!

Today, I am free from an Egyptian mindset!

I am released from a mindset that wants me to remain in mental bondage.

Today, I am free from a wilderness mindset!

I am released from a mindset that hinders me from reaching the promises of God!

Today, I am free from ungodly thoughts!

I am free from negative thinking, doubtful thinking, double-minded thinking, and restricted thinking!

Today, I will think outside of the box because my God is not contained, and neither is my thinking!

A HUMONGOUS God means I must have humongous thoughts!

Today, I am free from all sickness and illnesses that are polluting my body!

I am released from every illness (name the sickness)

that has attached itself to my bloodline!

Today, I am free from depression!

I am released from all symptoms of generational roots that are attached to depression!

Today, I am free from oppression!

I am released from the grips, holds, and the weights associated with the spirit of oppression!

Today, I am free from heartache!

I am released from unforgiveness, regret, guilt, and the heartache of those who have done me wrong!

Today, I am free from procrastination!

I am released from an inconsistent, undetermined, and hesitant mindset!

Today, I am free from stagnation!

I am released from a stagnated mind, a stagnant will, and every stagnant opposing force that keeps me from moving forward!

Today, I am free from weariness!

I am released from frustration, stress, disappointment, sorrow, and any unknown symptoms related to weariness!

Today, I am free from heaviness!

I am released from the extra pressure that rests on me!

Today, I am free from brokenness!

I am free from every broken cycle in my life. Right now, everything is being restored!

Today, I am free from false burdens!

I am released from everything that is not of my Heavenly Father, everything that is a lie, and everything that does not concern me. I am no longer burdened down by false burdens, In Yeshua's Name, Amen.

Today, I am free from ungodly relationships!

I am released from ungodly friendships, acquaintances, and connections!

Today, in Jesus' Name, I am totally set free!

And it is so. Amen.

DATE___/____/_____

JOURNAL & NOTES

"Then I will give you rain in due season,
and the land shall yield her increase,
and the trees of the field shall yield their fruit."
-Leviticus 26:4

_____

_____

_____

_____

_____

_____

_____

_____

_____

_____

_____

_____

today is: MONTH of _____ YEAR _____
day 1 2 3 4 5 6 7 8 9 10 11 12 13 14 15 16 17 18 19 20 21 22 23 24 25 26 27 28 29 30 31

PRAYER
is your
PERSONAL
KEY to
heaven
BOYD K. PACKER

Today I am grateful for:

prayer journal

I have seen the
Hand of God
in my life today

pray for:

Day 05

BREAKING UP FALLOW GROUND

"Sow to yourselves in righteousness, reap in mercy; break up your fallow ground: for it is time to seek the LORD, till He come and rain righteousness upon you." -Hosea 10:12

A Rhema Word from The Lord

I come as a Gardner to prepare your heart for the harvest. I cannot, nor will plant or rain on fallow ground. I come to gather the thorns in your heart, pluck the unrighteous weeds that have grown, and dislodge any stubborn rocks.

I come to place your heart in the Refining Fire to burn off everything that is not pleasing to Me.

I am preparing your **spirit**.

I am preparing your **heart**.

I am preparing you for **miracles.**

I am preparing you for **signs and wonders.**

I am preparing you for the **rain!**

I am preparing you for **my blessings** *said, The LORD*

DATE___/____/_____

JOURNAL & NOTES

*"For I will pour water upon him that is thirsty,
and floods upon the dry ground: I will pour my
spirit upon
thy seed, and my blessing upon thine offspring."*
-Isaiah 44:3

_____

_____

_____

_____

_____

_____

_____

_____

_____

_____

_____

today is: MONTH of _____ YEAR _____

day 1 2 3 4 5 6 7 8 9 10 11 12 13 14 15 16 17 18 19 20 21 22 23 24 25 26 27 28 29 30 31

PRAYER
is your
PERSONAL
KEY *to*
heaven
BOYD K. PACKER

Today I am grateful for:

I have seen the
Hand of God
in my life today

pray for:

prayer journal

Day 06

SPIRITUAL ALIGNMENT

"You shall also decree a thing, and it shall be established for you: and the light shall shine upon you always." -Job 22:28 NASB

{Decree means: An official order issued by a legal authority.

Declare means: To make known formally, officially, or explicitly.

Remember, you have been given the authority to decree.}

Prophetic Declaration

Today, I decree and declare in the Name of Yeshua, physical healing, mental healing, emotional healing, and spiritual healing for myself and those connected to me.

I come into alignment with **Isaiah 53:5, my Father's Word states: "He was wounded for my transgressions, He was bruised for my iniquities: the chastisement of my peace was upon him, and by his stripes, I AM HEALED!"**

Today, I decree and declare that my thoughts come into alignment with **Colossians 3:2: "Think on things above and not beneath!"**

Today, I decree and declare that my steps are walking into full alignment with **Psalm 32:23: "The steps of a good man/woman are ordered."**

I decree and declare that I am in alignment with divine open doors according to **Deuteronomy 28:6: My Father says, "I am blessed when I come in and blessed when I go out!"**

I decree and declare that all of my needs are in alignment with **Philippians 4:19: "For my God, will supply all my needs according to His riches in Glory through Christ Jesus!"**

Today, I decree and declare that every lack in my life come into alignment with **Psalm 34:10: LORD, You said, "I will lack no good thing!"**

My finances have been on the wrong side of the road, going in the wrong direction for too long. My finances have been going left, but today I decree and declare that my finances go right!

Galatians 3:28, states: "That if I belong to You, then I am Abrahams's seed, heirs according to the promise."

LORD, Your Word also says in **Psalm 35:27: "You have pleasure in the prosperity of Your servant."**

I align my thoughts, creative ideas, business plans, checking, and savings account with Your Promise in **Deuteronomy 8:18: "For it is He that giveth me the power to get wealth, that He may establish his covenant,"**

"The blessing of the LORD, it maketh rich, and he addeth no sorrow with it." -Proverbs 10:22

Today, I decree and declare that I am a lender and not a beggar or a borrower according to Your Word in **Deuteronomy 15:6, which states: "I will lend and not borrow!"**

Heavenly Father, Your Word declares in Deuteronomy 28:13, You will make me "the head and not the tail, above only and not beneath!"

I decree and declare the holes in my pockets are stitched up because I have considered Your Ways and not my own!

I decree and declare the plans of God in **Jeremiah 29:11, "will overrule in my life and grant me the promise of an expected end!"**

I decree and declare the seeds I planted spring up and produce a bountiful harvest according to **2 Corinthians 9:6: "He which soweth sparingly shall reap also sparingly, and he which soweth bountifully shall reap also bountifully."**

Today, I decree and declare that victory belongs to me according to **1 Corinthians 15:57: "My Father has given me the victory through Our Lord Jesus Christ!"**

In Jesus' Name, I decree and declare. Amen.

DATE____/____/_____

JOURNAL & NOTES

"Then shall we know, if we follow on to know the LORD: his
going forth is prepared as the morning; and he
shall come unto us as the rain, as the latter and
former rain unto the earth." -Hosea 6:3

_____

_____

_____

_____

_____

_____

_____

_____

_____

_____

today is: MONTH of _____ YEAR _____

day 1 2 3 4 5 6 7 8 9 10 11 12 13 14 15 16 17 18 19 20 21 22 23 24 25 26 27 28 29 30 31

PRAYER
is your
PERSONAL
KEY to
heaven
BOYD K. PACKER

Today I am grateful for:

I have seen the
Hand of God
in my life today

pray for:

prayer journal

Day 07

YOU CALLED ME

"I will give you the treasures of darkness and hidden wealth of secret places, so that you may know that it is I, the God of Israel, who call you by your name." – Isaiah 45:3

A Rhema Word from the Lord

{A message from the LORD to you.}

I have called you by your name.

I strategically, fearfully, and wonderfully created you.

I have ordered your steps and lightened your path.

You are the apple of My eye and the sheep of My pasture.

Delight in Me and I will give you the fullness thereof.

Turn not to weep with sorrow yet sing and rejoice.

I have heard your prayers, and I am swift to respond.

Seek not your way or your own understanding, but firmly stand on My Word.

Be assured that I have never left you, nor will I ever leave.

Allow My Voice to lead you through every dark place and My arms to carry you through the deep waters. You are my child, and I have called you by your name,

said The Lord.

DATE___/____/_____

JOURNAL & NOTES

"As the rain and the snow come down from heaven, and do not return to it without watering the earth and making it bud and flourish so that it yields seed for the sower and bread for the eater," - Isaiah 55:10, NIV

_____

_____

_____

_____

_____

_____

_____

_____

_____

_____

_____

today is: MONTH of _____ YEAR _____

day 1 2 3 4 5 6 7 8 9 10 11 12 13 14 15 16 17 18 19 20 21 22 23 24 25 26 27 28 29 30 31

PRAYER is your **PERSONAL KEY** to **heaven**

BOYD K. PACKER

Today I am grateful for :

prayer journal

I have seen the

Hand of God

in my life today

pray for :

Day 08

CALL ON MY NAME

"I will offer you a sacrifice of thanksgiving and call on the
Name of the Lord".-Psalms 116:17 -NLT

Today, I call upon Your Great Name. ABBA, I call You Father. I call You Daddy. I call You Omi-Present, Omni-Scient, and Omni-Potent, A Name that is above all names. A Name that the heavens and earth must obey! There is POWER in Your Wonderful and Marvelous Name!

Heavenly Father, You are the KING of kings, LORD of lords, and the GOD of all gods.

I call You, I AM, Alpha and Omega, the Beginning and the End, the Which Is, Which Was, and Which Is To Come.

LORD, You are the First and the Last.

You are my El Eloah, My God Who is Strong and Mighty!

Elohim, My God, Who is the Creator of all!

El Shaddai, The Almighty One!

I worship You, Adonai, because You are Lord!

You are Jehovah, The Great I Am!

You are Jehovah Jireh, My God Who Provides!

You are Jehovah Rapha, My God Who Heals!

You are Jehovah Nissi, my Banner, and I raise You on high, LORD!

You are Jehovah M'Kaddesh, My Lord Who Sanctifies!

You are Jehovah Shalom. You Are my Peace in the time of turmoil!

You are Jehovah Elohim. You Are The Lords of Lords, and besides You, there is no other!

Jehovah Tsidkenu, My Lord of Righteousness!

Jehovah Shammah, My God that is Always There!

You are Jehovah Sabaoth. You are the Lord of Host!

Oh, El Elyon, You Are the Most High God!

You are El Roi, My God that sees all!

El Olam, From Everlasting to Everlasting, You are my God!

El Gibhor, You Are a Mighty Warrior, and nothing is too hard for You! Who is this King of Glory? The LORD strong and mighty, the Lord mighty in battle.

LORD, bless Your Holy Name!

You are my Jehovah Rohi, "The Lord is my Shepard and I shall not want. He makes me to lie down in green pastures. He leads me beside the still waters. He restores my soul. He leads me in the paths of righteousness for His name's sake.

Yea, though I walk through the valley of the shadow of death, I will fear no evil: for You are with me; thy rod and thy staff they comfort me.

You prepare a table before me in the presence of mine enemies:

You anoint my head with oil; my cup runs over.

Surely goodness and mercy shall follow me all the days of my life: and I will dwell in the house of the LORD forever." Amen.

DATE___/___/_____

JOURNAL & NOTES

"Neither say they in their heart, Let us now fear the LORD our God, that giveth rain, both the former and the latter, in His season: He reserveth unto us the appointed weeks of the harvest." -Jeremiah 5:24

_____

_____

_____

_____

_____

_____

_____

_____

_____

_____

_____

_____

_____

today is: MONTH of _____ YEAR _____

day 1 2 3 4 5 6 7 8 9 10 11 12 13 14 15 16 17 18 19 20 21 22 23 24 25 26 27 28 29 30 31

PRAYER is your PERSONAL KEY to heaven

BOYD K. PACKER

Today I am grateful for:

I have seen the
Hand of God
in my life today

pray for:

prayer journal

Day 09

WHOSE REPORT WILL YOU BELIEVE?

"Who hath believed our report? and to whom is the arm of the Lord revealed?" – Isaiah 53:1

{It's one thing to say something, but it requires faith to believe it. Today, I need you to believe the report of the LORD because that's the only Word that works by faith.}

Whose report will I believe? I will believe the report of the LORD is true.

Today, I believe every word that you have spoken about me, and not what the enemy speaks.

I believe Your word will not return to You void.

I believe my circumstances are changing!

I believe my season is shifting!

I believe nothing shall be impossible for me!

I believe the Lord has given me the strength to do all things!

I believe Your Grace is sufficient!

I believe Your Mercy is renewed daily!

I believe all things will work together for my good!

I believe whatever I ask, it shall be given!

I believe You will never leave or forsake me!

I believe the blind shall see, the deaf will hear, and the cripple will walk!

I believe everything that's dry in my life will be restored by Your Holy Power!

Today, I believe my circumstances are shifting from not enough to more than enough!

LORD, I believe that All Your Promises are Yes and Amen.

In Yeshua's Name, I pray. Amen.

DATE___/____/_____

JOURNAL & NOTES

"Nevertheless, he left not himself without witness, in that he did good, and gave us rain from heaven, and fruitful seasons, filling our hearts with food and gladness."
-Acts 14:17

_____

_____

_____

_____

_____

_____

_____

_____

_____

_____

today is: MONTH of _____ YEAR _____

day 1 2 3 4 5 6 7 8 9 10 11 12 13 14 15 16 17 18 19 20 21 22 23 24 25 26 27 28 29 30 31

PRAYER
is your
PERSONAL
KEY to
heaven
BOYD K. PACKER

Today I am grateful for:

prayer journal

I have seen the
Hand of God
in my life today

pray for:

Day 10

A DAY OF REFLECTION

"This is the day which the LORD *hath made; we will rejoice and be glad in it."-Psalm 118:24*

Congratulations S.I.C., you made it to the 10th day!

You have been throwing out the old things to prepare for the new!

This is a perfect day to reflect on the goodness of our Heavenly Father. As you may know, the number 10 signifies completeness in divine order. It also represents the ending of an old cycle and the beginning of something new. Hallelujah!

I'm sure you can agree that this 10th day is much different than the day you first started. By now, you should be feeling a portion of the shifting. If not, please make sure you're following the instructions that were given. Your faith, boldness, and power in strategic prayers are going to help shift and change the atmosphere in your life.

Quick question: Have you been journaling after each prayer? If so, this is a perfect day to sit back and reflect on your writings from the last 9 days.

During your writings today,

1. I would like you to explain how you feel now, compared to 9 days ago.

2. Take a moment and reflect on the Goodness of God.

3. Give yourself some credit, reflect on the goodness inside of you.

DATE___/____/_____

JOURNAL & NOTES

"Who giveth rain upon the earth, and sendeth waters upon the fields:" -Job 5:10

_____

_____

_____

_____

_____

_____

_____

_____

_____

_____

_____

_____

today is: MONTH of _____ YEAR _____

day 1 2 3 4 5 6 7 8 9 10 11 12 13 14 15 16 17 18 19 20 21 22 23 24 25 26 27 28 29 30 31

PRAYER is your PERSONAL KEY to heaven

BOYD K. PACKER

Today I am grateful for:

prayer journal

I have seen the

Hand of God

in my life today

pray for:

Day 11

REMEMBER

"Remember the former things of old: for I am God, and there is none else; I am God, and there is none like me."
- Isaiah 46:9

A Word from the Lord

Remember, it is I who held your hand and walked you through the darkest hours.

It is I who captured every teardrop.

Remember, it is I who felt your deepest pain.

It is I who held back the high winds that tried to knock you down.

Remember, it is I who caught you before you stumbled and fell.

When faced with the many challenges of life, remember, it is I who caused My Peace to prevail.

Remember, it is I who had the final answers to every question.

Remember, it is I who continues to uphold you with My Righteous right hand.

Remember, It Is I Who Still Is And Forever Will Be, said the Lord.

DATE____/____/_____

JOURNAL & NOTES

"Then said the LORD unto Moses, Behold, I will rain

bread from heaven for you; and the people shall go out and gather a certain rate every day, that I may prove them..." -Exodus 16:4

_____

_____

_____

_____

_____

_____

_____

_____

_____

_____

_____

today is: MONTH / _____ YEAR _____

day 1 2 3 4 5 6 7 8 9 10 11 12 13 14 15 16 17 18 19 20 21 22 23 24 25 26 27 28 29 30 31

PRAYER
is your
PERSONAL
KEY to
heaven
BOYD K. PACKER

Today I am grateful for:

I have seen the
Hand of God
in my life today

pray for:

prayer journal

Day 12

GOD OF ZION

"I am the Lord the God of all mankind. Is anything too hard for me?"-Jeremiah 32:27

{It is inhumanly possible to change ourselves without the help and guidance of the Almighty God} – T.J.

My LORD of Zion, I know that nothing is too hard for You. I also know that You have the ability to change the wrong within me and make it right. Only You can change what I don't have the power to change myself.

LORD, I'm asking You to renew a right spirit in me, make me clean, and make me whole. You did it in the ancient days, and I know You can do the same for me today.

LORD, create in me a great warrior like David and bless me with the willpower to encourage myself in You.

Grant me strength like Samson in the natural and spiritual. LORD give me the strength to face and overcome every obstacle and hurdle that is set before me.

LORD, bless me with wisdom like Solomon. Your Word says that, if anyone lacks wisdom, let them ask. Father, I humbly ask for wisdom, the wisdom that supersedes my natural ability, thinking, speaking, and understanding.

Father, cover me with favor like Esther, according to **Psalm 5:12, "For thou, LORD, wilt bless the righteous with favour and You will cover me as *with* a shield."**

LORD, trust me with prosperity like Job. ABBA, forgive me for not always being faithful in the little you have given me. Forgive me for the times I mismanaged the things You entrusted with me. LORD, I desire to be faithful in a little so You can trust me with much.

LORD, I know my safety is in You, so I grab hold of the horns on the altar.

Like Jacob, LORD, I won't let go! I won't let go until you bless me! LORD, change my name and give me a new walk.

LORD, increase my substance, bless my first fruit, and bind the mouths of every demonic insect that is continually trying to eat up that which I have planted.

At this very moment, I am standing firmly on Your promise in **Joel 2:25 that states: "I will restore to you the years that the locust hath eaten, the cankerworm, and the caterpillar, and the palmerworm."**

Heavenly Father, allow the POWER in Your Mighty hands to be manifested in my life!

In Yeshua's Name, I ask. Amen.

DATE____/____/_____

JOURNAL & NOTES

"Do any of the worthless idols of the nations bring rain? Do
the skies themselves send down showers? No, it is you,
LORD, our God. Therefore, our hope is in you, for you are
the one who does all this."
-Jeremiah 14:22, NIV

_____

_____

_____

_____

_____

_____

_____

_____

_____

today is: MONTH / _____ YEAR _____
day 1 2 3 4 5 6 7 8 9 10 11 12 13 14 15 16 17 18 19 20 21 22 23 24 25 26 27 28 29 30 31

PRAYER
is your
PERSONAL
KEY to
heaven
BOYD K. PACKER

Today I am grateful for:

prayer journal

I have seen the
Hand of God
in my life today

pray for:

Day 13

POWER WORDS

"Death and life are in the power of the tongue: and they that love it shall eat the fruit thereof" -Proverbs 18:21

The tongue has the power of life and death, and those who love it will eat its fruit". - NIV

{Do you know your words are like seeds? Every time you speak a word, whether good or bad, a seed is being planted in your life and the lives of others; therefore, you must be very careful of the words that you choose to speak.} - Tammy Jae

Heavenly Father, forgive me for not always being careful of my choice of words. Blessings and curses should not come out of the same mouth.

Today, I call back and destroy, in the Name of Yeshua, every corruptible, rotten, and fruitless seed that I have planted by speaking words that destroy, instead of speaking words that give life.

LORD, You have given me the power to speak death or life with my words, and from this day forward, I choose to speak life.

Today, I choose to plant seeds that will produce good fruit and bring peace and grace to the ears of those who listen.

I choose to speak words of life into my own life.

I choose to speak life into others.

I choose to speak life into every lifeless and dry situation.

I choose to bless and not curse.

I choose to build up and not tear down with my words.

I choose to plant and not uproot with my words.

LORD, I know now that I will eventually eat the word seeds that I speak, whether good or bad, life or death.

Father, today, I choose to speak words of hope, peace, strength, love, and encouragement.

Most of all, LORD, I choose to speak words that will bring you Honor, Praise, and Glory.

In Yeshua's Name, I pray. Amen.

DATE___ / ____ / _____

JOURNAL & NOTES

"The LORD will send rain at the proper time from his rich treasury in the heavens and will bless all the work you do." – Deuteronomy 28:12, NLT

today is: MONTH of _____ YEAR _____
day 1 2 3 4 5 6 7 8 9 10 11 12 13 14 15 16 17 18 19 20 21 22 23 24 25 26 27 28 29 30 31

PRAYER is your **PERSONAL KEY** to **heaven**
BOYD K. PACKER

Today I am grateful for:

prayer journal

I have seen the
Hand of God
in my life today

pray for:

NOTE TO THE READER

Over the next several days, you will see a slight difference in how the prayers are structured. There will be several blank spaces. These blank spaces are available for you to fill in the blanks and personalize the prayer. After you fill in the blanks, pray the prayer with POWER and BOLDNESS!

Day 14

JERICHO WALLS

"On the seventh day, the Israelites got up at dawn and marched around the town as they had done before. But this time they went around the town seven times.

The seventh time around, as the priests sounded the long blast on their horns, Joshua commanded the people, "Shout! For the Lord has given you the town. - v. 15

When the people heard the sound of the rams' horns, they shouted as loud as they could. Suddenly, the walls of Jericho collapsed, and the Israelites charged straight into the town and captured it." – v. 20 -Joshua 6:15, 20, NLT

{Did you know there's power in your "Shout?"}

LORD, I thank You because a powerful "Shout" can knock down walls! Today, I shout down the Jericho walls in my life, and I take full possession of my promises!

Today, I Shout down every wall surrounding my heart that I have built!

Today, I Shout down the walls in my_____!

Today, I Shout down the walls surrounding_____!

Today, I Shout down the walls that are separating_____!

Today, I Shout down the walls_____!

Today, I Shout down the walls preventing me from_____!

Today, I Shout down the walls_____!

Today, I shout down the walls_____!

In the Name of Jesus, I command every wall to come down.

Amen.

DATE___ / ____ / _____

JOURNAL & NOTES

God, You poured out abundant rain on your inheritance.
When Israel was weary, you sustained her.
-Psalm 68:9, ISV

_____

_____

_____

_____

_____

_____

_____

_____

_____

_____

_____

_____

today is: MONTH of _____ YEAR _____
day 1 2 3 4 5 6 7 8 9 10 11 12 13 14 15 16 17 18 19 20 21 22 23 24 25 26 27 28 29 30 31

PRAYER
is your
PERSONAL
KEY *to*
heaven
BOYD K. PACKER

Today I am grateful for:

I have seen the
Hand of God
in my life today

pray for:

prayer journal

Day 15

DRY PLACE

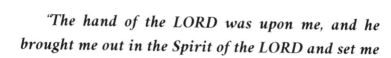

"The hand of the LORD was upon me, and he brought me out in the Spirit of the LORD and set me down in the middle of the valley: it was full of bones.

And he led me around among them, and behold, there were very many on the surface of the valley, and behold, they were very dry.

And he said to me, "Son of man, can these bones live?" And I answered, "O Lord GOD, you know."

Then he said to me, "Prophesy over these bones and say to them, O dry bones, hear the word of the LORD.

Thus, says the Lord GOD to these bones: Behold, I will cause breath to enter you, and you shall live". – Ezekiel 37 1-5, ESV

{There are times in our lives when things will dry up. The above scripture gives an example of how we can speak life into any dead situation and cause those dead & dry things (marriage, business, finances, etc.) to live again.}

Today, I speak life to every lifeless situation, rain to the drought, and sun to the storm!

Today, I burn the roots of every anti-Christ spirit that tries to steal, hinder, or deactivate my prophetic voice! I will not back down, I will not be quiet, I will stand firm, and I will prophetically speak over my life. In the Name of Jesus.

Right now, I speak life into every dry place that needs rain from Heaven!

I call forth fresh wind to every dark and dry place in my life. Today, I speak life into_____!

Today, I speak life into _____!

Today, I speak life into _____!

Today, I speak life to _____!

Today, in the Name of Jesus, I shall live and not die and declare the works of the LORD!

Today, I speak life to _____!

Today, I speak life to _____!

Today, I speak life to _____!

And it is so, in Jesus' Name. Amen.

DATE___ / ____ / _____

JOURNAL & NOTES

"For the earth which drink in the rain that cometh oft upon it, and bringeth forth herbs meet for them by whom it is dressed, receive blessings from God." - Hebrews 6:7

_____

_____

_____

_____

_____

_____

_____

_____

_____

_____

today is: MONTH of _____ YEAR _____
day 1 2 3 4 5 6 7 8 9 10 11 12 13 14 15 16 17 18 19 20 21 22 23 24 25 26 27 28 29 30 31

PRAYER is your PERSONAL KEY to heaven
BOYD K. PACKER

Today I am grateful for:

prayer journal

I have seen the
Hand of God
in my life today

pray for:

Day 16

FAVOR

"Surely, LORD, you bless the righteous; you surround them with your favor as with a shield." - Psalm 5:12, NIV

LORD, I am grateful for Your undeserving favor that covers me like a shield. I thank You for favor, not because of something spectacular I did, but because of how Spectacular You Are.

Today, I thank You for favor in

_____!

I thank You for favor in

_____!

I thank You for favor!

_____!

Thank You, for favor!

_____!

Thank You for favor

_____!

Thank You for favor in advance in

_____!

Thank You for blessing me with favor in my

_____!

Thank You for unfailing favor

_____!

Thank you for your unseen favor

_____!

Thank You for favor with You and
people_____ !

Thank You because Your anger is for a moment, but
Your fa-vor is for a lifetime

_____!

Thank you for unbreakable and unshakeable favor

_____!

In Jesus' Name. Amen!

DATE___/____/_____

JOURNAL & NOTES

"He covers the heavens with clouds, provides rain for the earth, and makes the grass grow in mountain pastures." – Psalm 147:8

_____

_____

_____

_____

_____

_____

_____

_____

_____

_____

_____

_____

today is: MONTH of _____ YEAR _____

day 1 2 3 4 5 6 7 8 9 10 11 12 13 14 15 16 17 18 19 20 21 22 23 24 25 26 27 28 29 30 31

PRAYER is your PERSONAL KEY to heaven
BOYD K. PACKER

Today I am grateful for:

prayer journal

I have seen the
Hand of God
in my life today

pray for:

Day 17

PRAY FOR OTHERS

"And the LORD *turned the captivity of Job when he prayed for his friends: also, the* LORD *gave Job twice as much as he had before." -Job 42:10*

Day 16, Wow! First, I want to commend you for pressing. I know some days may have been a little rough, but nevertheless, you've pressed on.

Today, I am going to elaborate briefly on the importance of praying for others. Foremost, praying for someone is not optional; it is mandatory. In fact, Jesus is sitting on the right hand of the Father interceding/pleading on our behalf daily (Romans 8:34), so if the Son of God intercedes, why shouldn't we? As Believers, we cannot get so consumed in our own issues that we forget to pray and intercede for others. Actually, it's quite selfish to be concerned only about our well-being.

The scripture states in John 15:13, *"Greater love hath no man than this, that a man lay down his life for his friends."*

Oftentimes, this scripture is taken totally out of context. The scripture is not suggesting that you die for your friend, but it is merely stating, there is no greater love, than when you lay down your own situations of life and care enough to pick up someone else's issues. Too often, we get so overwhelmed in our own circumstances that we forget about what the next person might be going through.

The heading scripture shows us the results of Job laying down his many issues and caring enough to pray for his friends. As you can see from reading the scripture, Job's life changed drastically when he stopped focusing on himself. My friend, I encourage you today and the days ahead to stop focusing on your problems and pray for someone, just as Job did.

DATE____/____/_____

JOURNAL & NOTES

I will send rain for your land at the right time. I will send the autumn rain and the spring rain. Then you can gather your grain, your new wine, and your oil. – Deuteronomy 11-14, ERV

_____

_____

_____

_____

_____

_____

_____

_____

_____

_____

_____

_____

today is: MONTH ⁄ _____ YEAR _____

day 1 2 3 4 5 6 7 8 9 10 11 12 13 14 15 16 17 18 19 20 21 22 23 24 25 26 27 28 29 30 31

PRAYER
is your
PERSONAL
KEY *to*
heaven
BOYD K. PACKER

Today I am grateful for :

I have seen the
Hand of God
in my life today

pray for:

prayer journal

Day 18

BREAKTHROUGH SEASON

*"God will stand up and breakthrough in their presence. Then they will pass through the gate, going out by it. Their king will pass in front of them with the L*ORD *at their head". -Micah 2:13, NLT*

Prophetic Declaration

LORD, I thank You for Peace, Strength, Wisdom, Increase, and Provision to bring everything that You have placed inside of me into fruition!

Today, I decree and declare recovery for everything that was lost, stolen, or withheld. In the Name of Jesus!

I decree and declare shackles are loosed, obstacles are removed, roadblocks are demolished, chains are broken, and straps are cut loose, so I may freely walk into my appointed breakthrough season. In the Name of Jesus!

Today, I decree and declare that everything *(specifically name those things that have been held up)*_____ in my life that has been held in captivity is now set free in Jesus' Name!

Today, I come in the authority of Jesus Christ, bombarding the entryway to my breakthrough, and I slay every demonic giant blocking my entrance with the same strength David used to slay Goliath.

I decree and declare that my Breakthrough Door is wide open, blockage free, and awaiting my entrance!

Today, I am a Champion!

I am a Warrior!

I am Victorious!

I am an Overcomer!

I am a Winner!

Father, I embrace my turnaround season with open arms, a renewed mind, and a sincere heart! LORD, I thank You in advance for an open heaven, open floodgates, open doors, open windows, divine connections, divine relationships, and divine appointments!

LORD, I thank You for the one YES that overruled the many "No!"

I Thank You because many others will be blessed due to my Breakthrough!

Today, I accept the release of Your Fresh Oil and New Rain to walk gracefully into my Appointed Breakthrough Season. In Jesus' Miraculous Name, I pray. Amen!

DATE___ /____ /_____

JOURNAL & NOTES

"He directs the snow to fall on the earth and tells the rain to pour down." –Job 37:6, NLT

_____

_____

_____

_____

_____

_____

_____

_____

_____

_____

_____

_____

_____

_____

_____

today is: MONTH / _____   YEAR _____

day 1 2 3 4 5 6 7 8 9 10 11 12 13 14 15 16 17 18 19 20 21 22 23 24 25 26 27 28 29 30

PRAYER
is your
PERSONAL
KEY *to*
heaven
BOYD K. PACKER

Today I am grateful for :

I have seen the

Hand of God

in my life today

pray for :
_____
_____
_____
_____
_____
_____
_____
_____
_____
_____
_____
_____

Day 19

DAY OF WORSHIP

"Those who blew the trumpets and those who sang were like one person. They made one sound when they praised and thanked the Lord. They made a loud noise with the trumpets, cymbals, and instruments of music. They praised the Lord, singing, "The Lord is good. His faithful love will last forever."

"Then the Lord's Temple was filled with a cloud.

The priests could not continue to serve because of the cloud, because the Glory of the Lord filled the Temple." - 2 Chronicles 5:13-14, ERV

Do you know Heaven is waiting on a specific sound?

Allow me to share some insight with you.

Did you know that God only responds to your worship and not your complaints?

Did you know that you are not waiting for God to respond, but God is waiting on your response?

God is waiting to hear a certain sound from you. He is waiting for your praise.

The scripture clarifies in Psalm 22:3 that **God inhabits the praises of His people**, which means He will come and dwell among His people during their worship to Him.

Did you know that your earthly worship signals heaven and alerts Abba that you're calling? And guess what? When you call, He answers, and when Abba enters into your atmosphere, everything must shift.

Let's briefly examine two relevant scriptures, beginning with Saul in 1 Samuel 16:23. Whenever a tormenting spirit would bother (torment) Saul, he called for David, and when David arrived, he worshipped with his instrument, and the tormenting spirit went away. You see, Saul was being tormented, but everything changed when David worshipped God because torment, chaos, confusion, or anything else that is unrighteous cannot stay when the Presence of God enters in.

My second point is: David was a prophet (Acts 2:30), and he worshiped prophetically through his music, which caused a mighty atmosphere shift. S.I.C., I need you to understand this. *Prophetic worship, prophetic prayers, and prophetic declarations* will shift any atmosphere. Now, you may be saying, "But, I'm not a prophet." Well, allow me to show you what the scriptures state in Joel 2:28: *"I will pour out my Spirit on all flesh and your sons and daughters will prophesy."*

Side note: Before I go any further, I want to make sure we are on the same page with a basic understanding of how the prophetic operates. I am not stating that every believer walks in the office of a prophet. However, if you are a Holy Spirit-filled believer, you are authorized to speak prophetically over your own life. You may be wondering, but how can I prophesy over my own life?

First, here is a better understanding of the prophetic:

- The Prophetic office carries a greater level of authority.

- You must first be called by God. (Jeremiah 1:5)

- Trained. (1 Samuel 19:18- 20)

- Ordained. (Acts 14:23) to speak fluently and accurately into the lives of others.

- There are times when God will speak through a "Believer" who does not have a prophetic gift, but that does not make that person a prophet

Humbly, I walk in the office of a prophet, which means God has chosen and equipped me to be His mouthpiece on the earth; therefore, I speak exactly what God instructs me to say, or I speak what He shows me through vision and dreams. He uses me to warn people of things to come, encourage people of things to come, and help churches move in the direction that He has intended for His church to go.

The roles of a prophet differ, but this is my current assignment. There are different levels in the prophetic realm, but the level of prophetic authority that I am currently speaking of, is for every Believer; however, this level of prophetic authority will only work in your own life and not someone else's life.

The authority to speak prophetically into another's life has been given to a "Believer" who operates as a prophet because they have been gifted to be the voice of God.

I am reiterating on this because I do not want anyone randomly trying to prophesy into another person's life without having the proper authority or permission from God.

If you pray/prophesy against God's Will on someone's behalf, or against that person's own will, it is considered witchcraft, and I call it "prophet-lying".

Therefore, we must always pray according to God's Will *(You can find out His Will in the Bible and through a consistent prayer life)*.

Jesus stated in Luke 22:42, ***"Father, if you are willing, please take this cup of suffering away from me. Yet I want your will to be done, not mine."***

For example, you can pray for healing, deliverance, etc. in another's life because all those things are within God's Will.

Side note: If you would like to learn more about the "do's and don'ts" of the prophetic, please read my book, "Behind The Mask" by Tammy Jaé, on Amazon.

Now, back to you, believers can prophesy by speaking things that are not into how you would like them to be according to the will of God. This means you are simply speaking your future into your present. That is what prophecy is, and this is how prophecy operates for every believer. Take a look at the scriptures below,

"Then Jesus said to the disciples, "Have faith in God. I tell you the truth, <u>you can say to this mountain</u>, 'May you be lifted up and thrown into the sea,' and it will happen."

"But you must really believe it will happen and have no doubt in your heart. I tell you, you can pray for anything, and if you believe that you've received it, it will be yours."
–Mark 11:22-24, NLT

The above scripture states that *"<u>you can say to this mountain</u>"* this means, you already have the authority to speak, change, and remove a situation (mountain) or anything that resembles a mountain out of your life. Here's the catcher, you have been authorized to remove some things and call some things forth. Hallelujah!

"Let us come before his presence with thanksgiving and make a joyful noise unto Him with psalms." - Psalms 95:2

Unlike any other day, I need you to press into an intimate worship with the Father. Exalt and express to

Abba how Marvelous He is and tell Him what He really means to you. Tell God how much you love and adore Him.

S.I.C, don't hold back. I need you to shout a high praise unto the Lord!

Release a praise from your heart that will get heaven's attention. Praise is what God desires to hear because we were created for God's glory (Isaiah 43:7). Being in the presence of God's Glory is a wonderful experience. No one should ever be the same afterward. It's an encounter like none other.

In the midst of your worship, I need you to begin prophesying over yourself. Start by speaking what God says about you. Speak your words in a future tense and not a present tense.

For example, speak *"I am healed!"* instead of saying *"I'm going to be healed."*

In Genesis, the Bible states that the earth was without form, void, and dark, and God said, ***"Let there be light!"*** There was light because God spoke the "light" into existence. He did not say it was going to be light. Just as God called "light" into existence, He has given His children the ability to speak things into existence in our lives.

Don't forget to write about today's experience with the LORD!

DATE___/____/_____

JOURNAL & NOTES

"Ask the Lord for rain in the spring,
for he makes the storm clouds.
And he will send showers of rain so every field
becomes a lush pasture." – Zechariah 10:1

_____

_____

_____

_____

_____

_____

_____

_____

_____

_____

today is: MONTH of _____ YEAR _____

day 1 2 3 4 5 6 7 8 9 10 11 12 13 14 15 16 17 18 19 20 21 22 23 24 25 26 27 28 29 30 31

PRAYER
is your
PERSONAL
KEY to
heaven
BOYD K. PACKER

Today I am grateful for:

I have seen the
Hand of God
in my life today

pray for:

prayer journal

Day 20

THE SHIFT

"And when the day of Pentecost was fully come, they were all with one accord in one place."

"And suddenly there came a sound from heaven as of a rushing mighty wind, and it filled all the house where they were sitting." -Acts 2:1-2

On the day of Pentecost, a mighty shifting took place. A rushing wind shifted the atmosphere and has changed the lives of countless generations. Father, I thank You because that same sound of a rushing mighty wind resides within me, which makes me an atmosphere shifter!

Today, I shift the atmosphere with a shifted mindset!

Today, I shift the atmosphere by shifting the words I speak!

Today, I shift the atmosphere by shifting my voice from fearful to fearless!

Today, my situation has shifted because my praise has shifted! Today, I shift my _____!

Today I shift the _____!

Today I shift _____!

Today I shift _____!

Today I shift _____!

Today I shift_____!

Father, I thank You for the authority to shift_____!

In Jesus' Name. And it is so.

DATE___/____/_____

JOURNAL & NOTES

"He shall come down like rain upon the mown grass; as showers that water the earth." -Psalms 72:6

_____

_____

_____

_____

_____

_____

_____

_____

_____

_____

_____

_____

_____

_____

today is: MONTH of _____ YEAR _____

day 1 2 3 4 5 6 7 8 9 10 11 12 13 14 15 16 17 18 19 20 21 22 23 24 25 26 27 28 29 30 31

PRAYER is your PERSONAL KEY to heaven

BOYD K. PACKER

Today I am grateful for :

I have seen the Hand of God in my life today

pray for :

prayer journal

Day 21

THE SOUND OF RAIN

"And Elijah said unto Ahab, Get thee up, eat and drink; for there is a sound of abundance of rain." - 1 Kings 18:41

Father God, I hear the sound of abundance rain because I am speaking rain into my existence! Daily, I will walk by faith and not by sight, and even though I cannot physically see the rain, I can spiritually hear the rain! The sound of rain lets me know that the abundance of rain is closer than it appears.

I hear the sound of overflow!

I hear the sound of victory!

I can hear the sound of heaven moving on my behalf!

I hear the sound of the floodgates opening!

I hear the sound of keys rattling and doors unlocking!

Father, I hear the sound of the atmosphere shifting!

Abba, I hear the sound!

The sound lets me know that my breakthrough is near!

The sound is alerting me to position myself for the release of Your Blessings!

Lord, I will rise up and rejoice at the sound of the rain!

I will stand up and dance to the sound of victory!

I will raise my voice in adoration for the rain is falling!

Lord, I lift up clean hands to receive Your Abundant Rain!

In the Name of Jesus Christ. Amen!

DATE___/___/_____

JOURNAL & NOTES

"And I will make them and the places round about my hill a blessing; and I will cause the shower to come down in his season; there shall be showers of blessing."
-Ezekiel 34:26

_____

_____

_____

_____

_____

_____

_____

_____

_____

_____

_____

today is: MONTH of _____ YEAR _____

day 1 2 3 4 5 6 7 8 9 10 11 12 13 14 15 16 17 18 19 20 21 22 23 24 25 26 27 28 29 30 31

PRAYER is your **PERSONAL KEY** to **heaven**

BOYD K. PACKER

Today I am grateful for:

I have seen the *Hand of God* in my life today

pray for:

prayer journal

PROPHETIC RAIN

{A prophetic prayer specifically for you, my S.I.C. Tammy Jae}

I prophesy to you through the prophetic grace, authority, and mantle that has been gifted to me.

I call forth the Prophetic Rain in your life, and I prophesy that the rain of GOD's blessings shall fall and overtake you!

I prophesy that this is a season of a turnaround, a season of abundant favor, a season of victory, a season of more than enough, a season of expansion, a season of heights, and a season of depth!

I call forth the rain on your behalf, and I speak to every dry place to be filled with an abundance of rain!

I speak to every fruitful seed that you have planted, and I command it to come forth with a great harvest, in the Mighty Name of Yeshua!

I speak overflow in your life, home, and resources!

I speak to every void, and I command it to be filled!

I speak to every lifeless situation and I command it to breathe right now, in the Name of Jesus!

I speak to every wall that is blocking your victory, and I com-mand it to fall right now, in the Name of Jesus Christ of Nazareth!

I command every locked door to be divinely opened with your key of FAITH!

I command every deaf and blinding spirit to enter a dry and waterless place, so you may clearly see your purpose and loudly hear your destiny calling!

I speak Deuteronomy 45:8 over your life. "**The LORD shall command the blessing upon you in thy storehouses, and in all that you settest thine hand unto.**"

HEAVENLY FATHER, it is Your Will that those who are obedient to Your Word be blessed.

LORD OF HOST, I thank you for sending forth the rain!

Thank You, LORD, for raining your blessings on my sisters and brothers, Your children!

Thank You for raining in the lives of YOUR People, ABBA!

Father, thank You for new testimonies bursting forth and letting the praises of YOUR Glory Arise!

Today, I prophesy that every word I have spoken over your life will not fall to dry ground, but the rain of GOD will cause it to do everything that I have commanded by the Holy Ghost Power working within me!

Today, if you only believe it, you shall receive it!

And it is so, in Jesus' Name. Amen.

DATE___/____/_____

JOURNAL & NOTES

"I know your works. Behold, I have set before you an open door, which no one is able to shut. I know that you have but little power, and yet you have kept my word and have not denied my name."
-Revelation 3:8 ESV

_____

_____

_____

_____

_____

_____

_____

_____

_____

_____

today is: MONTH of _____ YEAR _____

day 1 2 3 4 5 6 7 8 9 10 11 12 13 14 15 16 17 18 19 20 21 22 23 24 25 26 27 28 29 30 31

PRAYER *is your* **PERSONAL KEY** *to* **heaven**
BOYD K. PACKER

Today I am grateful for:

prayer journal

I have seen the *Hand of God* in my life today

pray for:

DATE___ /____ /_____

JOURNAL & NOTES

_____

_____

_____

_____

_____

_____

_____

_____

_____

_____

_____

_____

_____

_____

Author's Bio

Tammy Jaé is an Ordained Minister, Prophetess, Mentor, Founder/CEO of One Faith Publishing, Sisterhood International Ministry (a Facebook support group for women nationwide), and an avid speaker.

Tammy Jaé is on a mission to help Believers execute biblical game plans to become victorious in health, wealth, deliverance, and so forth.

She is a native of Michigan but currently resides in the Virginia area with her husband and children.

ABBREVIATIONS/DEFINITION

Prophet – nataph, (naw-taf) to pour down; gently fall, drip; to drip word, preach, prophesy. -Hebrew, Strong Concordance

KJV, King James Version

ESV, English Standard Version

ISV, International Standard Version NASB, New American Standard Bible NIV, New International Version NLT, New Living Translation

Made in the USA
Coppell, TX
18 September 2022